Quick & Easy Ba... ets

6 Crochet Patterns with Step-by-Step Photos

Tara Cousins

Copyright © 2013 Tara Cousins

www.TigerRoadCrafts.com

All rights reserved.

Contents

This collection of small stroller-size baby blankets works up quickly. Using a large size N/9.00mm crochet hook and two strands of worsted weight yarn means a thick & cozy blanket that is easy to complete in half the time! Skill level ranges from beginner to easy intermediate.

Pattern Notes:

- ➢ Directions between ** are meant to be repeated.
- ➢ Directions between ( ) are meant to be worked into one stitch.
- ➢ Loose ends can be worked in as you crochet or woven in at the end with a yarn needle.
- ➢ The main centers of each baby blanket are worked using a large size N/9.00mm crochet hook and two strands of yarn. When working with two strands, complete each crochet stitch as if you had one strand, but hold both strands together.
- ➢ To use two strands from the same skein, see photo at right. Each skein of yarn has an "inner" and an "outer" strand. Use both of these at once.

Working with two strands from one skein

Working the foundation chain with double strands

Foundation Chain

All crochet items begin with a simple slip knot and a foundation chain. The pattern will begin by stating how many chains (abbreviated ch) are needed.

Slip knot   *Chain*

Once you have a foundation chain, you can work your stitches back along that chain. Crochet is a series of loops. The loops are stitches which begin by hooking through the loops on either the foundation chain or on other stitches. Sometimes you will use chains in the middle of a pattern. Each loop is counted as one stitch.

The single crochet stitch (abbreviated sc) is the most basic stitch. To complete a **single crochet**, insert the hook in either both loops, front loop only, or back loop only (as pattern indicates). Draw up new loop, pull yarn through both loops.

Turning Chain (tch)

Crochet items are worked in either rounds or rows. Often, there is a combination of both. For example, these baby blankets are worked in rows first and then finished with border rounds.

When working in rows, an extra chain is needed at the end of each row. This gives you enough room to turn the work and start a new row.

Single Crochet (sc)

Step 1: insert hook

Step 2: pull up a loop

Step 3: pull through both loops

Completed single crochet

For single crochet rows (sc), complete one turning chain.

For double crochet rows (dc), complete either two or three turning chains (depending on the pattern and the looseness of your chains).

Turning chain with sc

The double crochet stitch is taller and looser than a single crochet.

To complete a **double crochet**, wrap yarn around hook once, insert hook into loops indicated, pull up yarn. Now you have three loops. Pull through two loops. Pull through remaining two loops.

When working in rounds, you will often need to turn corners. If it is a regular 90 degree corner, complete three stitches in each center corner stitch. This increases the stitches enough so that the work will lie flat.

Turning a corner in sc and dc

Double Crochet (dc)

Step 1: yarn over hook

Step 2: insert hook

Step 3: pull up a loop

Step 4: pull through two loops

Step 5: pull through last two loops

Changing Colors

You can change colors at the end of a row in two ways. First, you can bring in the new color as the final pull-through of the last stitch. Another option is using the turning chain as a way to bring in the new color.

Color change option #1

Color change option #2

Note: when the color will be used again soon, you do not need to cut the yarn between rows. Simply keep the yarn attached and bring up from previous rows when needed. The border will hide the yarn along the edge of the blanket.

Weaving in Loose Ends

Loose ends (such as when you start, end, or change colors midway through a project) can be worked in as you crochet or they can be woven in afterwards with a yarn needle. Use the needle to hide the tails within the work, and trim the excess. I find that weaving the

tails in this manner holds them hidden more effectively that working them in as you go. It is also much easier for the beginning crocheter.

Attaching Appliqués

Some of the designs have additional crocheted motifs which are attached to the main project (motif is another word for appliqué, or something sewn on at the end). First, follow the instructions to make the motif. Make sure you leave a long enough yarn tail. Next, use a yarn needle and the long tail to sew the motif directly onto the project.

To create a double-sided look, two motifs are sandwiched around the project and may be attached simultaneously or individually.

Abbreviation List

ch	Chain
Sl st	Slip stitch
tch	Turning chain
sk	Skip
rnd	Round
sc	Single crochet
dc	Double crochet
ldc	Long double crochet
Dc3tog	Double crochet 3 sts together
Dc4tog	Double crochet 4 sts together
Dc7tog	Double crochet 7 sts together
Rsc	Reverse single crochet
Rhdc	Reverse half double crochet

Cotton Candy

Skill Level: Easy

Finished size: 24" x 36"

Materials:

Red Heart Super Saver yarn in the following colors: Lemon (250 yds), Baby Pink (300 yds) and Pale Orchid (300 yds). Also used is Hobby Lobby's *I Love This Yarn* in Pistache (600 yds). For simplicity, colors in pattern are referred to as yellow, pink, purple and green.

Size N/9.00MM crochet hook

Yarn needle

Gauge: 4" = 8 sts and 10 rows of the long double crochet pattern

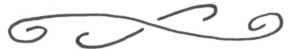

Special Stitch: Long Double Crochet (ldc)

Yarn over hook (1), insert hook into stitch directly 2 rows below (2), pull up a loop(3), pull through two loops(4), pull through last two loops(5).

| 1 | 2 | 3 | 4 | 5 |

Blanket Center:

To begin, with two strands of green (held together), ch 42.

Row 1: sc in 2nd ch from hook and each ch across, for a total of 41 sc. Ch 1, turn.

Row 2: sc in each st across.

At the end of row 2, in the last pull through of the last stitch, drop green strands (keep connected to blanket – do not cut) and pull in a double strand of yellow. Ch 1, turn.

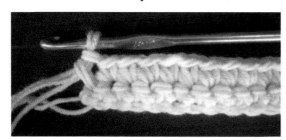

End of row 2

Note: Only cut the yarn strands at the end of the rows when that color will not be used again for more than a few rows. Bring up yarn loosely along the edge when needed. The border row will disguise yarn at edges of blanket.

Row 3: *sc, ldc* repeated acros, ending with sc in last st. Ch 1, turn.

Row 3

Row 4: sc in each st across. Connect green strands (pull up from row below) in the last pull through of the last stitch. With green, ch 1, turn.

Row 5: 2 sc. *Ldc, sc* repeated across, ending with sc in the last st.

Row 5

Row 6: sc in each st across. Connect yellow strands (pull up from row below) in the last pull through of the last stitch. With yellow, ch 1, turn.

Row 7: *sc, ldc * repeated across.

Row 7

Rows 8- 85: Continue stitch pattern. Switch colors according to the attached color chart. At the end of each row, ch 1, turn.

For all even rows: sc in each st across.

For odd rows: alternate sc, ldc. Always begin and end with a sc.

Close up view of the blanket side

The blanket is made up of a total of 85 rows, ending with a green row. At the end of row 85, tie off. Using a yarn needle, weave in any loose ends.

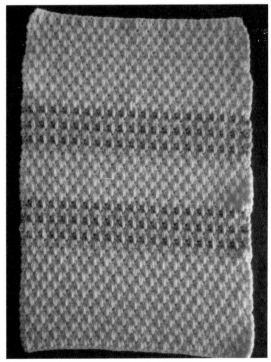

View of completed blanket center

Border:

Use two strands of pink, and connect with a chain along top corner of blanket.

Rnd 1: with pink, 3 sc in corner st, sc in each st across top edge of blanket. 3 sc in next corner st. Along rough edge of blanket, work sc so that stitches are spaced evenly and blanket lies flat. To do this *work 4 sc (one per row) then skip a row* repeated down side edge. Make sure to work the sc around the yarn strands on the sides of blanket to hide them.

Beginning border round 1

sc along rough side edge of blanket

3 sc in next corner st, sc in each st along bottom of blanket, 3 sc in last corner st. Work sc along side edge as before. Sl st to first st in round, ch 1, turn.

Rnd 2: sc in each st around, working 3 sc in each of the four corner stitches. At end of round, sl st to first st in round, tie off.

Beginning of border round 3

Beginning of round 2

*Step 1: insert hook into stitch to the **right** of hook*

View of completed border round 2

Round 3: The last round on the border is worked with 2 strands of purple yarn.

Connect purple to any stitch on edge of blanket. *ch 1, skip 1 stitch, Rsc* repeated around. See photo steps.

Step 2: Pull up a loop – new loop is to the left of the first loop

Step 3: pull through both loops – Rsc complete

No need to do anything special around the corners

At the end of the border round 3, sl to first st, and tie off.

Chain 1, skip next st, and repeat

Working border round 3

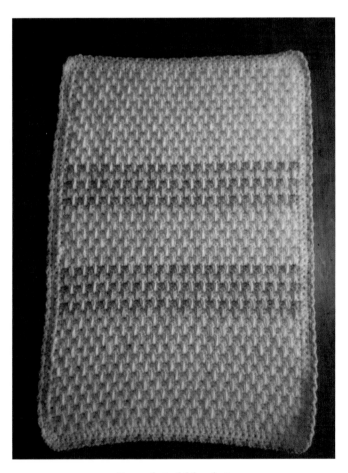

Completed blanket

Color Chart

Each color band represents **two** rows.

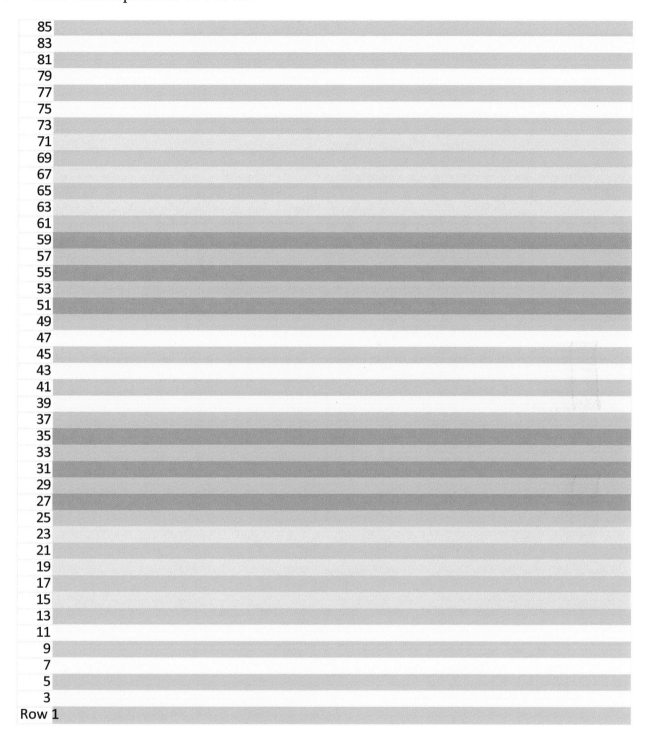

85
83
81
79
77
75
73
71
69
67
65
63
61
59
57
55
53
51
49
47
45
43
41
39
37
35
33
31
29
27
25
23
21
19
17
15
13
11
9
7
5
3
Row 1

Spring Rainbow

Skill Level: Easy

Finished size: 21" x 26"

Materials:

Red Heart Super Saver yarn in the following colors: Buff (500 yds), Cornmeal (200 yds), Orchid (200 yds), Aruba Sea (250 yds), Baby Pink (200 yds) and Amethyst (250 yds). For simplicity, colors in pattern are referred to as brown, yellow, light purple, teal, pink and dark purple.

Size N/9.00MM crochet hook

Size I/5.50MM crochet hook

Yarn needle

Gauge: 4" = 10 sts and 4 rows of the double crochet ripple pattern.

Special Stitch:

Double Crochet 3 together (dc3tog): yarn over hook, insert into st indicated, pull up a loop. Yarn over hook again, and insert hook into next st, pull up a loop. Yarn over again, insert hook into next st, pull up a loop. Now there are 4 loops on hook (8 with double strands). Pull through all loops on hook. This makes 3 stitches combine into 1.

Blanket Center:

To begin, with one strand of brown and one strand of yellow (held together as in photo below), ch 43. **Note:** Each row in the main blanket is worked with one strand of brown and one strand of another color.

Row 1: dc in 3nd ch from hook. *3 dc, dc3tog (worked over 3 chains), 3 dc, 3 dc in next ch* repeated across, ending with 2 dc in last ch.

Beginning of row 1

At the end of row 1, drop yellow (keep connected– do not cut) and pull in a new strand of light purple along with the brown, as a ch 1. This ch 1 connection serves as a tch. Turn.

Bringing in light purple – End of row 1

Note: Do not cut the yarn strands at the end of the rows. Keep yarn attached and bring up loosely when needed in later rows. The border row will disguise yarn at edges of blanket.

Row 2: with brown and light purple, **ch 2. Dc in first dc, *3 dc, dc3tog, 3 dc, 3 dc in next dc* repeated across. End with 2 dc in tch.** At the end of row 2, drop purple and bring in a new strand of teal along with the brown as a ch 1. Turn.

Bringing in teal – End of row 2

Row 3: with brown and teal, repeat stitch directions from row 2 (directions are in bold type). At the end of row 3, drop teal and bring in a new strand of pink along with the brown as a ch 1. Turn.

Bringing in pink - End of row 3

Row 4: with pink and brown, repeat stitch directions from row 2. At the end of row 4, drop pink and bring in a new strand of dark purple along with the brown as a ch 1. Turn.

Bringing in dark purple – End of row 4

Row 5: with dark purple and brown, repeat stitch directions from row 2. At the end of row 5, drop dark purple and bring up the strand of yellow that is still attached to the blanket. Bring yellow in with the brown as a ch. Turn.

Bringing up yellow – End of Row 5

Rows 6- 25: Repeat the stitch directions – each row is the same. Switch colors according to the pattern: (yellow/brown, light purple/brown, teal/brown, baby pink/brown, dark purple/brown), switching colors at the end of each row. Turn blanket at the end of each row.

Close up view of stitches

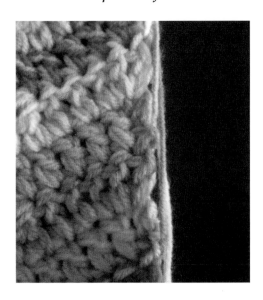

Close up view of blanket side

The blanket is made up of a total of 25 rows, ending with a dark purple/brown row. At the end of row 25, tie off. Trim off yarn. Using a yarn needle, weave in loose ends.

View of completed blanket center

Border:

Use two strands of yarn (from your one skein), and connect with a chain along top corner of blanket.

Rnd 1: with teal, 3 sc in corner st, sc in each st across top edge of blanket.

Beginning border round 1

3 sc in next corner st. Along rough edge of blanket, work sc so that stitches are spaced evenly and blanket lies flat. Work sc around yarn strands on the sides of blanket to hide them.

Working sc along rough side edge of blanket

3 sc in next corner st, sc in each st along bottom of blanket. 3 sc in last corner st. Work sc along side edge as before. Sl st to first st in round, ch 1, turn.

Rnd 2: sc in each st around, working 3 sc in each of the four corner stitches. At end of round, sl st to first st in round, tie off.

View of border round 2

Rnd 3: The last round on the border is worked with a size I/5.50MM hook and 1 strand of dark purple yarn.

Connect dark purple to any stitch on edge of blanket. In each stitch around work: (sc, dc, sc). This border round will make blanket ruffle slightly around the edges. No need to do anything differently around the corners, just work the stitches as indicated.

Completed border

Beginning of border round 3

At the end of the border round 3, sl st to first st, and tie off. Weave in all loose ends with a yarn needle and blanket is complete!

Skill Level: Easy

Finished size: 23" x 27"

Materials:

Red Heart Super Saver yarn in the following colors: Snow White, Baby Pink, Turqua, and Orchid. For simplicity, colors in pattern are referred to as white, pink, blue and purple. Less than 250 yds. of each color is needed.

Size N/9.00MM crochet hook

Size I/5.50MM crochet hook

Yarn needle

Gauge: 4" = 10 sts and 10 rows

Blanket Center:

All rows in the main center part of the blanket are worked with white and another color.

To begin, with 1 strand purple and 1 strand white (held together as in photo above), ch 53.

Row 1: sc in 4th ch from hook. *ch1, skip next loop, sc* repeated across, ending with a sc.

Beginning of row 1

Connect blue in tch at end of row 1. To do this, bring in blue as shown in photo below, adding to white and dropping the purple strand. Keep purple strand connected for later use. Turn.

Connecting blue in turning chain – end of row 1

Note: The white yarn strand is used in every row. Do not cut the colored yarn strands at the end of the rows. Keep yarn attached and bring up loosely when needed in later rows. The border row will disguise yarn at edges of blanket.

Row 2: with blue and white, *ch 1, sk sc st, sc in ch-1 space* repeated across, ending sc in tch space.

This stitch is often referred to as a seed stitch or a tweed stitch.

Beginning of row 2

At the end of row 2, connect pink yarn with a tch, dropping blue yarn. Turn.

Connecting pink in turning chain – end of row 2

Row 3: with pink and white, *ch 1, sk sc st, sc in ch-1 space* repeated across, ending with sc in tch space. At the end of row 3, bring up purple yarn and connect with a tch.

Beginning of row 3

Close up view of stitches

Bringing up purple yarn – end of row 3

Rows 4 - 60: Repeat pattern (purple/white, blue/white, pink/white), switching colors at the end of each row. Stitch directions for each row are the same: *ch 1, sk sc st, sc in ch-1 space* repeated across, ending with sc in tch space.

The blanket is made up of a total of 60 rows, ending with a purple row.

View after main center of blanket is completed

View of side edge

Using a yarn needle, weave in loose ends.

Border:

Connect two strands of purple with a chain along top corner of blanket. The first two border rounds are all single crochet.

Rnd 1: To begin, work 3 sc in the top corner stitch.

Then, working along top row, *sc in ch-1 space, sc in next st, sc in ch-1 space, skip 1 st* repeated across. Basically, work 3 sc then skip a stitch. This is so the blanket lays flat and stitches are spaced evenly.

Start of first border row

In next corner stitch, work 3 sc.

Along rough edge, work sc into each row: *3 sc, sk one row* repeated along edge.

Working along side edge

In next corner stitch, work 3 sc. Work bottom edge the same as top edge. Work 3 sc in last corner stitch. Along next side edge, work sc as before. Finish with a sl st to first sc in round.

Rnd 2: ch 1, turn. Sc in each st around, working 3 sc in each of the four corner stitches. Sl st to first st in round. Tie off.

Working border round 2

The third border round is worked with a smaller size I/5.50mm hook and only one strand of purple yarn.

Rnd 3: connect purple to the top corner stitch. *Work 5 dc into 1 stitch, sl st across next st, sl st across next st* repeated around.

Working border round 3

At the end of the border round 3, sl st to first st, and tie off. Weave in loose ends.

Heart Motif (make 2):

With pink, ch 3.

Note: at end of each row, ch 1, turn. Total number of stitches in each row is given in parentheses ( ).

Row 1: 2 sc across (2sc)

Row 2: 2 sc across (2sc)

Row 3: sc inc, sc inc. (4sc)

Row 4: sc across (4sc)

Row 5: sc inc, 2 sc, sc inc (6 sc)

Row 6: sc inc, 4 sc, sc inc (8 sc)

Row 7: sc across (8 sc)

Row 8: sc inc, 6 sc, sc inc (10 sc)

Row 9: sc inc, 8 sc, sc inc (12 sc)

Row 13: sc across (5 sc).

Row 14: 3 sc, sc dec (4 sc)

Row 15: 2 sc, sc dec (3st). Tie off.

New row 12 on other side of heart: connect pink to 6th stitch on row 11, according to photo below.

Row 10: sc across (12 sc)

Row 11: sc across (12 sc)

Row 12: 4 sc, sc dec (5 sc)

Row 12: sc dec, 4 sc (5 sc)

Row 13: sc across (5 sc)

Row 14: sc dec, 3 sc (4 sc)

Row 15: sc dec, 2 sc (3st). Tie off.

Attach blue to any spot on edge of heart. Sc around so that heart lies flat, working a sc decrease in center of heart. Sl st to first sc in round, tie off, leaving a long 20" tail to sew heart to blanket.

Repeat directions to make a second heart.

Attach heart: with the long blue yarn tail and a yarn needle, sew heart directly onto

blanket. Position according to photo below. Sew a basic running stitch and sew all around the outside blue edge of heart.

Sewing on heart

Sew a second heart on the direct opposite side of blanket in the same position. Hide stitches between the two hearts. Weave in all loose ends.

Project Complete!

Ocean Waves

Skill Level: Easy Intermediate

Finished size: 24" x 32"

Materials:

Red Heart Super Saver yarn in the following colors: Light Blue (color A), Aruba Sea (color B), Delft Blue (color C) and Real Teal (color D). For simplicity, the colors in the pattern are referred to by the letters A, B, C and D. About 250 yds. of each color is needed.

Size N/9.00MM crochet hook

Size J/6.00MM crochet hook

Yarn needle

Gauge: 4" = 12 sts and 4 rows of the wheel pattern.

Special Stitches:

Double crochet 4 together (dc4tog): yarn over hook, insert hook into st and pull up a loop. Yarn over again, insert hook into 2nd st and pull up a loop. Repeat two more times. Now you have 5 loops on hook (10 with double strands). Pull through all loops on hook. This combines 4 stitches into 1.

Double crochet 7 together (dc7tog): yarn over hook, insert hook into st and pull up a loop. Yarn over again, insert hook into next st and pull up a loop. Repeat five more times. Now you have 8 loops on hook (16 with double strands). Pull through all loops on hook. This combines 7 stitches into 1.

Blanket Center:

To begin, with 2 strands of color A (light blue) held together, ch 52.

Row 1: sc in 2nd ch from hook, sc in next ch *sk 3 ch, 7 dc in next ch, sk 3 ch, 3 sc* repeated across, ending with 2 sc.

Beginning of row 1

At the end of row 1, connect two strands of color B (Aruba Sea) in the tch. Bring in B as shown in photo below, dropping color A. Trim off color A. Turn.

Connecting color B in turning chain – end of row 1

Row 2: with A, ch 2. Dc4tog over the next 4 sts. *ch 3, 3 sc, ch 3, dc7tog over the next 7 sts* repeated across, ending with dc4tog over the last 4 sts. Ch 3, turn (see photos).

Dc4tog step 1

Dc4tog step 2

Dc7tog step 1

Dc7tog step 2

Row 3: still with color B, 4 dc in dc4tog stitch. *sk ch 3, 3 sc, sk ch 3, 7 dc in dc7tog* repeated across, ending with 4 dc in dc4tog. At the end of row 3, connect color C in tch. Turn. Trim off color B.

Beginning of row 3

Close up view of stitches

Row 4: with color C (Delft Blue), 2 sc. *ch 3, dc7tog over next 7 sts, ch 3, 3 sc* repeated across, ending with 2 sc. Ch 1, turn.

Rows 5 – 36: Rows 1 through 4 are repeated. Change colors according to guide below.

Row 5: C   Row 6: D   Row 7: D
Row 8: C   Row 9: C   Row 10: B
Row 11: B   Row 12: A   Row 13: A

View after row 13

Row 14: B   Row 15: B   Row 16: C
Row 17: C   Row 18: D   Row 19: D
Row 20: C   Row 21: C   Row 22: B
Row 23: B   Row 24: A   Row 25: A
Row 26: B   Row 27: B   Row 28: C
Row 29: C   Row 30: D   Row 31: D
Row 32: C   Row 33: C   Row 34: B

View of completed blanket center – rows 1-36

At the end of row 36, do not tie off color A. Keep attached to work the border.

Border:

Rnd 1: With color A, begin along top corner of blanket. Work 3 sc in corner st, sc in each st across top of blanket, 3 sc in the next corner st. Along rough edge of blanket, work sc stitches evenly so that blanket lies flat. 3 sc in next corner st, sc in each st along bottom edge, 3 sc in last corner st. Work sc along rough edge of blanket, again spaced evenly. At end of round, sl st to first st in round, ch 1, turn.

Beginning of border round 1

Working sc along rough side edge of blanket

Rnd 2: sc in each st around, working 3 sc into corner sts. At end of round, sl st to first st in round, ch 1, turn.

Rnd 3: repeat round 2. Tie off color A.

View after border round 3

Rnd 4: with 1 strand of color C and a size J/6.00MM crochet hook, connect to any st on the edge of blanket. Ch 3. 2 dc in first st, *sc in next st, 3 dc in next st* repeated around. At end of round, sl st to first st in round and tie off.

Beginning of border round 4

There is no need to do anything differently around the corners.

Working around a corner – border round 4

Weave in all loose ends with a yarn needle. Project Complete!

Easy Pastels

Skill Level: Beginner

Finished size: 21" x 26"

Materials:

Red Heart Super Saver yarn in the following colors: Aran, Light Blue, Cornmeal and Honeydew. For simplicity, colors in pattern are referred to as white, blue, yellow and green. About 250 yds of each color is needed.

Size N/9.00MM crochet hook

Yarn needle

Gauge: 4" = 10 sts and 10 rows

Blanket Center:

All rows in the main center part of the blanket are worked with white and another color.

To begin, with 1 strand green and 1 strand white (held together), ch 51.

Note: The white yarn strand is used in every row. Do not cut the colored yarn strands at the end of the rows. Keep yarn attached and bring up loosely when needed in later rows. The border row will disguise yarn at edges of blanket.

Row 1: sc in 2nd ch from hook. *ch1, skip next loop, sc* repeated across, ending with sc in last ch. Connect yellow in tch at end of row 1. Bring in yellow as shown, adding to white and dropping the green strand. Keep green strand connected for later use. Turn.

Connecting yellow in turning chain – end of row 1

Row 2: with yellow and white, sc, *ch1, sc in ch-1 space* repeated across, ending with a sc in last st. Connect blue yarn with a tch, dropping yellow yarn.

Beginning of row 2

Connecting blue in turning chain – end of row 2

Row 3: with blue and white, sc, *ch1, sc in ch-1 space* repeated across, ending with sc in last st. Bring up green yarn and connect with a tch.

Beginning of row 3

Bringing up green yarn – end of row 3

Repeat pattern (green/white, yellow/white, blue/white), switching colors at the end of each row.

The blanket is made up of a total of 59 rows, ending with a yellow row. Using a yarn needle, weave in loose ends.

View of side edge

Close up view of stitches

Border:

Connect two new strands of blue with a chain along top corner of blanket. The first border round is all single crochet.

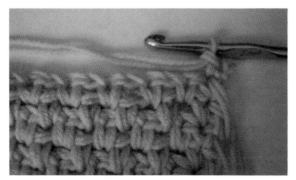

Attaching blue with a chain

Work 3 sc in the corner stitch. Then, working along top row, *sc, sc in ch-1 space, sc, skip ch-1 space* repeated across. Basically, work 3 sc then skip a stitch. This is so the blanket lies flat and stitches are spaced evenly.

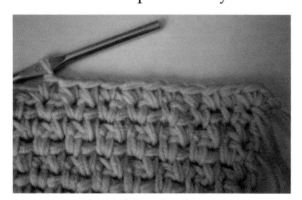

Start of first border row

In next corner stitch, work 3 sc. Along rough edge, work sc evenly so that blanket lies flat.

Working along side edge

In next corner stitch, work 3 sc.

Along bottom edge of blanket, *sc, sc in ch-1 space, sc, skip ch-1 space* repeated across.

Working along bottom edge

In next corner stitch, work 3 sc. Along rough edge, work sc as before.

Finish with a sl st to first sc in round, ch 1, turn.

Round 2 is worked as follows: *Rhdc, ch 1, skip next st* repeated around. However, when working around corners, do not skip a stitch. This will allow the blanket to lie flat.

The following photos will show the Rhdc (reverse half double crochet) step-by-step.

The Rhdc stitch is worked from **left to right**.

Yarn over hook

*Insert hook into stitch to the **right** of hook*

Pull up a loop

Pull yarn through all loops on hook

Chain 1. Skip next stitch and repeat.

Working Rhdc around blanket

At the end of the border round, sl to first st, and tie off. Weave in loose ends.

Personalized "Baby"

Skill Level: Beginner

Finished size: 21" x 26"

Materials:

Red Heart Super Saver yarn in the following colors: Spa Blue, Lemon and Frosty Green. For simplicity, colors in pattern are referred to as blue, yellow and green. Less than 250 yds. of each color is needed.

Size N/9.00MM crochet hook

Size I/5.50MM crochet hook

Yarn needle

Gauge: 4" = 10 sts and 10 rows

This blanket is very similar to the Easy Pastel Blanket. Personalize with a custom baby name!

Blanket Center:

To begin, with 2 strands of blue (held together), ch 51.

Row 1: sc in 2nd ch from hook. *ch1, skip next loop, sc* repeated across. Connect 2 strands of yellow in tch at end of row 1, dropping blue strands. Keep blue strands connected for later use. Turn.

Beginning of row 1

Connecting yellow in turning chain – end of row 1

Note: Do not cut the yarn strands at the end of the rows. Keep yarn attached and bring up loosely when needed in later rows. The border row will disguise yarn at edges of blanket.

Row 2: with yellow, sc, sc in ch1 space, *ch 1, sc in ch-1 space* repeated across. End with a sc in last st.

End of row 2

Connect green yarn with a tch, dropping yellow yarn. Turn.

Row 3: with green, sc, *ch1, sc in ch-1 space* repeated across.

Beginning of row 3

At the end of row 3, bring up blue yarn and connect with a tch. Turn.

Rows 4-55: Repeat color pattern: (blue, yellow, green), switching colors at the end of each row. Turn blanket at the end of each row.

For all odd rows: sc, *ch 1, sc in ch-1 space* repeated across.

For all even rows: sc, sc in ch-1 space, *ch 1, sc in ch-1 space* repeated across. End with a sc in last st.

Beginning of row 4

The blanket is made up of a total of 55 rows, ending with a blue row.

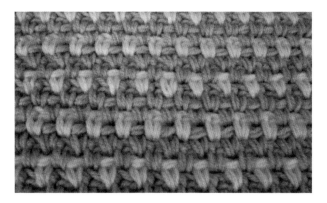

Close up view of stitches

At the end of row 55, tie off. Trim off green and yellow yarn. Using a yarn needle, weave in loose ends.

View after main center of blanket is completed

Border:

Connect two new strands of green with a chain along top corner of blanket. The first two border rounds are all single crochet.

Attaching green with a chain

Border rnd 1: work 3 sc in the corner stitch. Then, working along top row, *sc, sc in ch-1 space, sc, skip ch-1 space* repeated across. Basically, work 3 sc then skip a stitch. This is so the blanket lies flat and stitches are spaced evenly.

Start of first border row

In corner stitch, work 3 sc. Along rough edge, work sc spaced evenly.

View of side edge

In next corner stitch, work 3 sc. Work bottom edge the same way as top edge. Work 3 sc next corner st. Work rough edge as before. Finish with a sl st to first sc in round, ch 1, turn.

Border rnd 2: work sc in each st around, working 3 sc in each corner st. At end of round, sl st to first st in round. Tie off green.

Border rnd 3: the last round on the border is worked with a size I/5.50MM hook and 1 strand of blue yarn. The pattern is *Rsc, ch 1* repeated around.

The photos below will show the Rsc stitch step-by-step. The example below begins on stitch two of the border row to show the stitch more clearly.

The Rsc stitch is simply a single crochet worked backwards, from **left to right**.

Pull yarn through loops on hook

To work border, ch 1 and repeat

*Insert hook into the stitch to the **right** of previous stitch*

Working Rhdc around blanket

At the end of the border round, sl st to first st, and tie off. Weave in loose ends.

Pull up a loop

Completed border

Name Plate:

Use 1 strand of yarn and a size I/5.50MM hook.

For a three or four letter name, make a center green block of 13 stitches by 9 rows (instructions below). For a longer name, simply make a wider green block. Add an additional 4 stitches across per letter.

Row 1: With green, ch 14. Sc in 2nd ch from hook and each ch across.

Rows 2-9: sc in each st across. Ch 1, turn.

Tie off at the end of row 9, leaving a long tail to sew name plate to blanket.

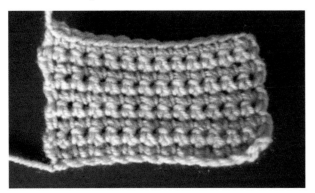

Completed green block

Border: with blue, connect to any stitch around the edge of green block. Work sc

around the edge, working 3 sc in each corner stitch. At the end of round, sl st to first st in round and tie off. Weave in ends.

Blue border

To form the name letters, make lengths of chains. Tie off chains, leaving long tails to sew onto blanket. It might take a few tries to figure out how big you would like your letters and how you would like them shaped.

The letters pictured were made as follows: b – 13 chains, a – 6 chains, b – 13 chains, y – 13 chains and 5 chains.

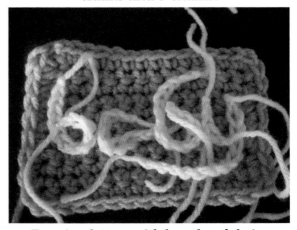

Forming letters with lengths of chains

Once you have enough lengths of chains, sew down the middle of chains with a basic running stitch. Tie off to the back of name plate and trim ends.

Sewing on letters

Positioning completed name plate

through the top layers only so that no sewing shows through the other side of blanket.

Project Complete!

Position the name plate onto blanket according to photo. Use the green yarn tail to sew onto blanket. Work a basic running stitch around the edge of the green block. Do not sew all the way through. The blanket is thick enough to work a running stitch

For additional information, free learn-to-crochet videos, free monthly patterns, and the complete collection of crochet patterns designed by Tara Cousins, visit

www.CuteKidsCrochet.com

Enjoy!

Printed in Great Britain
by Amazon